18th Century Superstar

Mozart

Georgia Beth

Consultants

Timothy Rasinski, Ph.D.
Kent State University

Lori Oczkus, M.A.
Literacy Consultant

Publishing Credits

Rachelle Cracchiolo, M.S.Ed., *Publisher*
Conni Medina, M.A.Ed., *Managing Editor*
Dona Herweck Rice, *Series Developer*
Emily R. Smith, M.A.Ed., *Content Director*
Stephanie Bernard/Susan Daddis, M.A.Ed., *Editors*
Robin Erickson, *Senior Graphic Designer*

The TIME logo is a registered trademark of TIME Inc.
Used under license.

Image Credits: Cover and p.1 (front) Carsten Koall/Getty Images,
(back) Glasshouse Images/Alamy Stock Photo; p.6 Ann Ronan Pictures/
Print Collector/Getty Images; p.9 DeAgostini/Getty Images; p.13
Illustration by Timothy J. Bradley; p.14 LOC [LC-DIG-pga-03844]; p.16
Apic/Getty Images; p.17 Igor Bulgarin/Shutterstock.com; pp.18, 25
FALKENSTEINFOTO/Alamy Stock Photo; p.21 World History Archive/
Alamy Stock Photo; p.27 Sean Gallup/Getty Images; all other images
from iStock and/or Shutterstock.

Library of Congress Cataloging-in-Publication Data

Names: Beth, Georgia, author.
Title: 18th century superstar : Mozart / Georgia Beth.
Description: Huntington Beach : Teacher Created Materials, 2017. |
Includes
  index.
Identifiers: LCCN 2016037451 (print) | LCCN 2016038171 (ebook) | ISBN
  9781493836314 (pbk.) | ISBN 9781480757356 (eBook)
Subjects: LCSH: Mozart, Wolfgang Amadeus, 1756-1791--Juvenile
literature.|
  Composers--Austria--Biography--Juvenile literature.
Classification: LCC ML3930.M9 B47 2017 (print) | LCC ML3930.M9
(ebook)|DDC
  780.92 [B] --dc23
LC record available at https://lccn.loc.gov/2016037451

Teacher Created Materials

5301 Oceanus Drive
Huntington Beach, CA 92649-1030
http://www.tcmpub.com

ISBN 978-1-4938-3631-4

© 2017 Teacher Created Materials, Inc.
Printed in China
Nordica.072018.CA21800845

Table of Contents

Cue the Orchestra

The lights dim. The conductor appears. The string players raise their bows in unison. A low note hums through the theater. The musicians. The singers. The audience. All eyes are on the conductor who is commanding every note.

Modern audiences tend to prefer other types of music over classical. It has a reputation for being **cerebral** and challenging. But attending a classical music concert can be a dramatic experience, and the music can provoke powerful emotions in listeners. Today, the greatest classical composers are **revered** as geniuses. To their **contemporaries**, they were also superstars. The emotions they evoked in listeners inspired wild adoration at performances around the world. Audiences loved the beauty and emotion of their novel compositions. And their rich works continue to affect people centuries later.

Hitting the High Notes

In the eighteenth century, Austria was a European center of politics, power, wealth, and culture. A new middle class began to afford some of the luxuries that before were only available to the aristocracy. This included leisure time, traveling to foreign countries, wearing the latest fashions, and attending concerts.

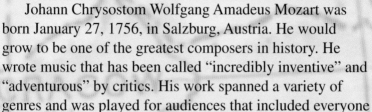

Johann Chrysostom Wolfgang Amadeus Mozart was born January 27, 1756, in Salzburg, Austria. He would grow to be one of the greatest composers in history. He wrote music that has been called "incredibly inventive" and "adventurous" by critics. His work spanned a variety of genres and was played for audiences that included everyone from King Louis XV to Johann Christian Bach. Today, the man behind these timeless pieces of music is known simply by a single name: Mozart.

Nuances of a Name

When he was baptized, his parents used the name Johannes Chrysostomus Wolfgangus Theophilus Mozart. In keeping with Catholic tradition, Johannes Chrysostomus is representative of the saint he is named for. He introduced himself as Wolfgang Amadé or Wolfgang Gottlieb. Today, we know him as Wolfgang Amadeus Mozart.

Prelude to Greatness

Philosophers have long asked whether it is nature or nurture that turns ordinary children into geniuses. Scientists look for evidence that genius is genetic. They study the early lives of their subjects. They hope to understand the early influences, motives, and challenges that shaped the **prodigies'** work. Studying the early life of Mozart may not provide all the answers, but it should help us understand the background of his musical genius.

Family Life

Mozart was the youngest of seven children. Only he and his sister, Maria Anna, survived past infancy. His father, Leopold, was a musician. He wrote *Treatise on the Fundamental Principles of Violin Playing*, a manual used to teach students how to play the violin. Mozart's mother, Anna, came from a middle-class family and was devoted to her children. Throughout his childhood, Mozart's home was filled with love and music.

Attending school was not a part of young Mozart's life. Like many children of the time, he never had a formal education. His father taught him arithmetic, history, and music. He also studied German, Italian, French, and Latin. But his lack of formal training became clear when he later moved through more educated circles or wrote letters home. He was famous for using his own **idiosyncratic** spelling and grammar.

Deconstructing Genius

True genius is about more than intelligence. It can't be measured with a test, and it's difficult to define. The term *genius* is most often used to describe someone, such as Mozart, who develops ideas that move a field of study forward in dramatic ways.

The First Stage Parent

As a musician, Leopold Mozart was proud of his children's talents. But he also used their talents to make money and become famous himself. He often looked for ways to ensure Wolfgang and Maria Anna would be able to perform for royalty and other influential people. Leopold pushed them to travel long distances to perform for wealthy audiences.

A True Prodigy

Surrounded by music, musicians, and instruments, Mozart began picking out notes on the keyboard at just three years old. The **wunderkind** listened intently during his sister's lessons. By the time he was five, he could play the pieces in her music books and had started **improvising** his own songs as well. Soon, he learned to play the violin. In time, Leopold began to take his son's talent even more seriously.

Music Therapy

Like artists and writers, musicians create to express their thoughts and feelings and make sense of the world. The effect is just as powerful on listeners. Listening to music can alter brain chemistry, support the immune system, reduce stress levels, elevate mood, promote healing, and more.

The prodigy enjoyed surprising audiences with his talent. He practiced playing blindfolded or with the keys covered. He showed off whenever the opportunity arose. Mozart charmed audiences with his spirited performances and took advantage of his young age by ignoring proper manners. Once, he even jumped on Empress Maria Theresa's lap and gave her a kiss. Not the manners expected at a royal performance!

Nannerl's Talent

Maria Anna, known as "Nannerl" by family and friends, may have been as talented as her more famous sibling. Her father once wrote, "My little girl plays the most difficult works which we have . . . with incredible precision and so excellently." She also composed her own music, though sadly, her compositions have been lost.

THINK LINK

◎ Do you think true genius can be identified early in life or only with the passage of time? Explain.

◎ What makes a musician a genius? Are these qualities different from those found in a scientist or a philosopher?

Playing with the Classics

Between 1763 and 1766, the Mozart family visited Munich, Stuttgart, Frankfurt, Brussels, Paris, London, and Amsterdam, among other cities. On the road, Mozart delighted at the chance to learn new musical styles. He studied other instruments and learned to sing. Like a poet who sprinkles foreign words into verse or a pun-loving writer, Mozart was eager to add to his musical vocabulary. He played with form and improvised new melodies. His new skills allowed him to write complete orchestras. It was an important milestone for the young composer.

Lost in Time

Mozart spent nearly a third of his life on the road, traveling to hear and perform music that couldn't yet be recorded and shared. Of course, at the time there were no mp3s, CDs, or even records to preserve performances. Contemporary musicians treasured every opportunity to watch one another play in person.

Mozart's Travels

Modern Music

As new instruments were invented, Mozart wrote to take advantage of the unique sounds they produced. The **harpsichord** was already common, but the piano only became popular in Mozart's time. He was one of the first composers to explore its dynamic possibilities, taking advantage of its ability to play both loudly and softly.

As Mozart grew older and was exposed to more music, his compositions become more complex. At first, he played a few notes on the harpsichord to see what sounds he liked. Then, he recorded his preferences on sheet music. As he became more experienced, he was able to hear the music in his head and write a song without playing a single note.

Eventually, the family traveled back to Salzburg. At age 13, Mozart played alongside his father in the court orchestra. Just three years later, he was named the concertmaster. The title was impressive but unpaid. Mozart's ambitious nature was not satisfied by the limited responsibilities of the position. He longed to branch out. He wanted to write operas, attract larger audiences, and become known as a composer.

I must climb the
highest mountain
and cross the
endless sea

Anatomy of an Opera

Mozart's greatest passion was writing operas. However, the composer is just one of many people needed to perform an opera. Let's take a look at how a modern opera is performed today.

The singers perform the songs and serve as the public faces of the opera. The diva is the main female singer in an opera company.

The musicians follow the conductor's lead, producing a powerful background for the singers.

The conductor leads the orchestra and makes sure the musicians stay in time with the singers.

The lighting and sound team use lights and sound effects to create the perfect mood for each scene.

The set designer creates the scenery, which helps the audience understand where the story takes place.

The stage manager works backstage to ensure everyone is where they need to be and all the costume, lighting, and set changes happen on time.

The composer develops the melody, working with singers and musicians to create the music in his or her head. The librettist writes the words that accompany the music in an opera. The term *libretto* means "little book."

The Music Swells

By the time he was 17 years old, Mozart could no longer use his reputation as a **plucky** prodigy to charm audiences. He was eager for independence from his father's influence. It was time to do the work that would be celebrated for centuries to come.

Mozart spent the next several years composing and studying the works of other composers. He received a small salary from the prince-archbishop and searched for ways to develop his talent. By age 20, he had produced more than 300 original compositions.

Spotlight on Song Structure

Mozart wrote many compositions, including sonatas, concertos, and symphonies. But what's the difference between these different types of compositions?

- Symphonies are pieces of music that are written in several sections, or **movements**. They are designed to be played by a large orchestra and draw on the sounds of a large range of instruments.

- Concertos are designed to help a soloist, accompanied by an orchestra, show off how brilliantly he or she can play.

- Sonatas are similar to concertos except that they may feature a soloist or a small ensemble accompanied by a piano. They are usually made up of two to four movements.

In 1777, he received his father's approval to travel with his mother in search of an orchestra for which he could compose. Along the way, he fell in love with a singer named Aloysia Weber. But he was not offered any work he felt was suitable to his talent. His mother grew ill and died in 1778, and a grief-stricken Mozart was disappointed to learn that Aloysia did not share his feelings. Mozart was without prospects of love or celebrity. Miserable, he returned to Salzburg.

In 1779, Mozart was made concertmaster and court organist. This time, the position was paid, although not extravagantly. He was furious when he was forced to eat and sleep with the servants. He longed to be famous for his work and celebrated for his talent, just as he had been as a child.

Salzburg, Austria

The Viennese Waltz

Slowly, Mozart found happiness. In 1782, he married Constanze Weber. Although he was once in love with her sister, he grew to love Constanze even more. Letters home show his affection for her. He addressed her as "dearest and best little wife" and wrote "2,999 and $\frac{1}{2}$ little kisses from me which are flying about, waiting for someone to snap them up." Later that year, the couple moved to Vienna, and soon after, Constanze gave birth to a baby boy.

A Low Note

Mozart wrote his *Jupiter Symphony* in 1788, but it is uncertain whether it was ever played during his lifetime. Today, this symphony is often found on recommended listening lists. It is now revered as one of his most complex symphonies.

A Tragic Time

Like so many families at the time, the Mozarts endured many tragic deaths that are now preventable by modern medicine. Sadly, most of Mozart's six children died shortly after birth. Only Karl Thomas and Franz Xaver Wolfgang survived into adulthood. When Mozart's father died in 1787, Mozart was devastated and overwhelmed.

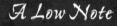

Constanze Weber

The first years in Vienna were difficult, as Mozart struggled to find work. His family suffered hardships and **estrangements**. But as he became more established, Mozart felt triumphant. He had found a city that suited him well, even calling Vienna "the land of the piano." It was a place where music was celebrated, and Mozart's compositions were popular with the royal audience. As his celebrity grew, his presence was in high demand. During one whirlwind month, he made appearances at more than 20 concerts. In time, he was **commissioned** to write operas, producing some of his most famous works while in Vienna, including *The Marriage of Figaro*.

scene from *The Marriage of Figaro*

Creative Interlude

Once Mozart became well regarded as a composer, he pushed himself to create more original pieces and to develop his own style. He wrote to please his audiences. But he also drew on his own **aesthetic** and strong technical skills to express a range of emotions. Musicians to this day consider his work bold and difficult. His work is fresh, modern, expressive, and personal. Many people consider his compositions to be musical descriptions of what it means to be human.

Everything from fairytales to **freemasonry** influenced Mozart. He wrote sonatas, chamber music, serenades, symphonies, and more. He helped popularize the piano concerto. Mozart wrote a large number of **masses** for the Catholic Church, but he was most passionate about writing operas. Invented in the 1600s, operas combined theater and music in dramatic ways that quickly became popular with audiences. Some were based on classic myths or legends, but many were love stories.

Formalizing the Catalog

In 1851, Ludwig von Köchel, an Austrian scholar, catalogued Mozart's music, giving each piece a number. These numbers are referred to as "Köchel numbers" and are still used when citing pieces of Mozart's music. Use this guide to decipher Mozart's catalog:

the song structure

the Köchel number

Piano Concerto No. 20 in D Minor, K 466

the instrument Mozart intended to be used to play this composition

the chronological order of the piece in relation to other piano concertos

Inspiring Ideas

In 1784, Mozart joined the masonic lodge, becoming a Freemason like many of his friends. Freemasons celebrated the ideals of the Enlightenment, which was a time when people began looking at the world through reason instead of religion. They organized meetings where scientists, scholars, artists, writers, and other thinkers could exchange ideas.

Everyday Genius

Mozart was well liked by his family, his friends, and royalty for his sense of humor and playful spirit. He often included funny songs and poems in his letters. And his personality was part of what drew royalty to him.

During his lifetime, anyone unfamiliar with his work may have believed he was more silly than serious about music. But his private letters to family and friends prove he worked hard. He loved music deeply. Once he said, "People err who think my art comes easily to me. I assure you, dear friend, nobody has devoted so much time and thought to compositions as I. There is not a famous master whose music I have not **industriously** studied through many times."

Prestissimo

Famous for his **prodigious** output, Mozart worked rapidly. He once wrote a sonata so quickly that he only had time to write the music for the violinist. At the premier, Mozart played the piano part with blank pages in front of him.

Reaching a Higher Octave

The great physicist and violin player Albert Einstein loved music and particularly admired Mozart's work. He once said Mozart's music "was so pure that it seemed to have been ever-present in the universe, waiting to be discovered by the master."

Many people assume writing music was effortless for Mozart based on the number of pieces he composed. But that may not have been the case. Whenever possible, he liked to do his creative work in the early morning. Sometimes he worked into the evening, if there wasn't a performance or concert to attend. It's difficult work creating something out of nothing, so Mozart made plenty of time for sleep and leisure. But he was also forced to devote many of his afternoons to teaching and administrative work. As it is for many artists, Mozart's creative process could be unpredictable. He sometimes put aside compositions and returned to them years later.

Mozart writing the overture for his opera, *Don Giovanni*, the night before its opening

Money Struggles

Mozart struggled to earn enough money to support his family. And even though he worked as a court musician, he didn't earn enough money to live like royalty. Private **patrons** sometimes commissioned music. In return, musicians such as Mozart would dedicate their work to a patron or to someone the patron loved. But these jobs were often uncertain. Sometimes Mozart gave music lessons, but it was difficult to make a good living with this work.

He did, however, make more than other musicians of the time. But there is evidence that he was not skilled at managing his money. He was eager for a court appointment that would fund a grand lifestyle for his family. Even his 800-**guilder** salary as the composer for the imperial court was not enough to support his extravagant dreams!

Mozart as Muse

The composer Ludwig van Beethoven is often compared to Mozart. He came to Vienna in 1787 and hoped to study with Mozart, who was 14 years his senior. But Beethoven was forced to return home when his mother died. Though he later returned to Vienna, he never had a chance to work with Mozart. Today, Beethoven and Mozart are both known for turning symphonies into the art form that is beloved by musicians.

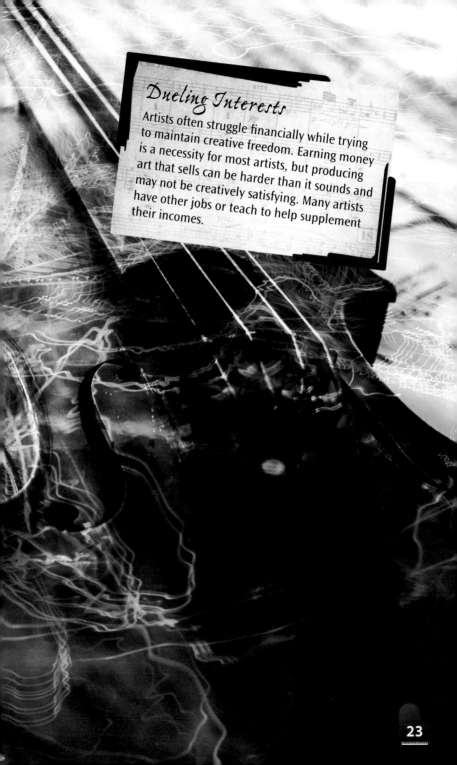

Dueling Interests

Artists often struggle financially while trying to maintain creative freedom. Earning money is a necessity for most artists, but producing art that sells can be harder than it sounds and may not be creatively satisfying. Many artists have other jobs or teach to help supplement their incomes.

Musical Flow Chart

Ready to hear the master at work? There's a Mozart song for every mood. Use this flow chart to find which pieces will hit a high note for you.

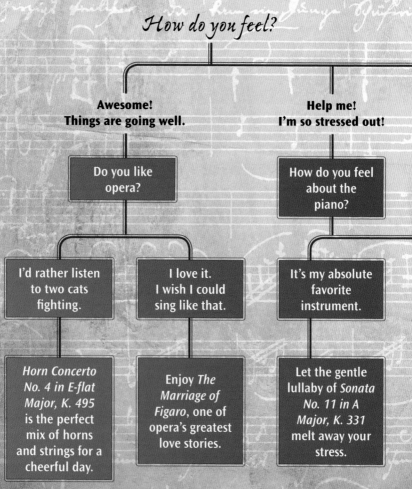

How do you feel?

Awesome!
Things are going well.

Help me!
I'm so stressed out!

Do you like opera?

How do you feel about the piano?

I'd rather listen to two cats fighting.

I love it. I wish I could sing like that.

It's my absolute favorite instrument.

Horn Concerto No. 4 in E-flat Major, K. 495 is the perfect mix of horns and strings for a cheerful day.

Enjoy *The Marriage of Figaro*, one of opera's greatest love stories.

Let the gentle lullaby of *Sonata No. 11 in A Major, K. 331* melt away your stress.

Eh.
I've been better.

Do you prefer vocals
in classical music?

I could live
without it.

No way!
Classical should
be strictly
instrumental.

Absolutely.
Vocals convey
more emotion.

*String Quartet
No. 12 in B-flat
Major, K. 172*
will make you
feel relaxed and
clearheaded in
no time.

Console your
sadness with
*Adagio and
Fugue in C
Minor, K. 546.*

Curl up with
*Requiem in D
Minor, K. 626*
when you're
feeling down.

Al Fine

In 1791, at the age of 35, Mozart was writing some of his most mature work, including the opera *The Magic Flute*. Tragically, that same year, he grew ill and died. Constanze worked to catalogue his work and preserve it for the public. His apprentice Franz Xaver Süssmayr completed an unfinished **requiem**. The piece had been commissioned by a mysterious patron, but Mozart believed the music was meant for him, saying "I know I have to die . . . I write [the requiem] for myself."

When he died, Mozart was widely admired as the greatest composer of his day. His work challenged musicians, singers, and audiences to understand music in new ways. Mozart wrote more than 40 symphonies, 27 concertos, 22 operas, and hundreds of other pieces. Centuries later, his work is still played regularly. Musicians of all ages continue to look to his playful, **eloquent** compositions for inspiration.

Reprising Greatness

In 2014, musicians began Mozart 250. This is a series of concerts that feature each of Mozart's major works in the order in which they were composed. The performances will take place over 27 years. The final performance will be in 2041, the 250th anniversary of Mozart's death.

The Magic Flute

Mozart's last opera tells the story of a handsome prince who rescues the girl he loves. But the symbols in the opera give it a deeper meaning about the quest for enlightenment. The aria sung by the Queen of the Night is one of the best known—and most difficult—in opera.

Coda

Joy. Grief. Wonder. Fear. Mozart's compositions **evoke** the full spectrum of human emotions. His **legacy** lives on in his music, which still connects with listeners today. **Musicologists** admire his melodies, citing them as technically flawless, yet even more stunning for their effortless quality, with each note perfectly chosen and irreplaceable. No more. No less. Exactly what any artist hopes for his or her work.

Glossary

aesthetic—relating to art or beauty

cerebral—related to the mind rather than feelings; intellectual rather than emotional

commissioned—paid a fee to someone for performing a service as directed

contemporaries—people who live at the same time as another person

eloquent—clearly showing feeling or meaning

estrangements—relationships that have become distant or no longer friendly

evoke—to bring a feeling to mind

freemasonry—the principles of Freemasons, a group of men who have secret rituals, help each other, and share ideas about enlightenment and wisdom; also known as *masonry*

guilder—a unit of money formerly used in the Netherlands

harpsichord—an instrument resembling a piano that has strings that are plucked

idiosyncratic—an unusual way in which a particular person behaves or thinks

improvising—speaking, creating, or performing without preparation

industriously—working very hard

legacy—something passed down from an ancestor

masses—sets of ceremonial songs and words for worship in religious churches, especially Catholic churches

movements—self-contained parts or sections of a longer musical composition

musicologists—people who study music

patrons—people who give money and support to artists or organizations

plucky—having or showing courage or determination

prodigies—young people who are unusually talented in some way

prodigious—impressive; amazing

requiem—a religious ceremony or piece of music for someone who has died

revered—showed great respect for someone

wunderkind—someone who achieves success or shows great talent at a young age

Index

Check It Out!

Books

Johnson, Paul. 2013. *Mozart: A Life*. Viking Books.

Meyer, Carolyn. 2008. *In Mozart's Shadow: His Sister's Story*. Harcourt Children's Books.

Sadie, Stanley. 2005. *Mozart: The Early Years 1756–1781*. W. W. Norton & Company.

Wates, Roye E. 2010. *Mozart: An Introduction to the Music, the Man, and the Myths*. Amadeus Press.

Wolff, Virginia Euwer. 2007. *The Mozart Season*. Square Fish.

Videos

"The Genius of Mozart." 19 March 2004. James Kent. BBC.

Websites

Bio. *Wolfgang Mozart: Biography*. http://www.biography.com/people/wolfgang-mozart-9417115.

Mozart: Child Genius. http://www.mozart.com.

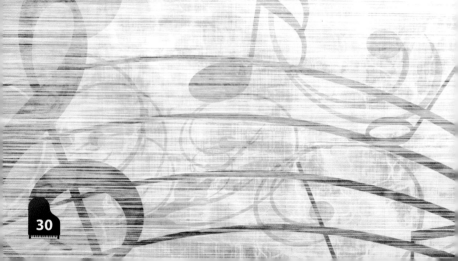

Try It!

Amadeus Mozart could play multiple instruments and composed amazing music in his head. Put yourself in Mozart's shoes and become a composer. First, you'll need to create a unique instrument and decide how it should be played. Then, compose your own song using your instrument.

- ◎ First, raid the recycling bin and art closet! Find materials that will help you create a musical instrument on your own. You might want to look for boxes, plastic, rubber bands, paper clips, and paper.

- ◎ Use the materials to craft an instrument that can make sounds. Try to create something that can produce more than one sound.

- ◎ Test your instrument to discover all the different sounds it can make. Combine those sounds to make a tune and practice playing your new composition.

- ◎ Once you have a catchy tune, write a few words to sing along.

- ◎ Finally, put it all together by singing your lyrics while playing your tune!

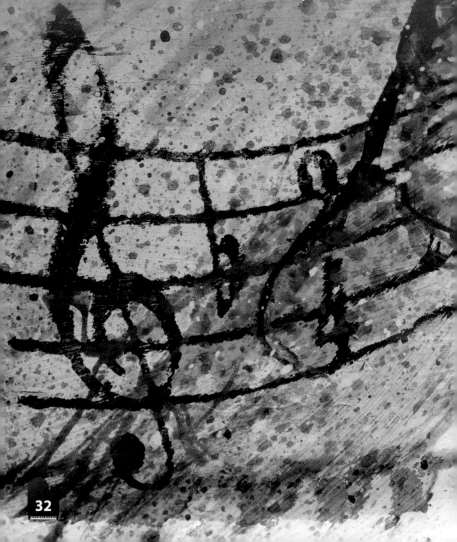

About the Author

Georgia Beth lives in Massachusetts with her husband, who indulged her Mozart obsession by listening to song after song with her during the writing of this book. Georgia is a writer, editor, and music lover who listens to everything from modern kirtan to pop. She treasures having her grandmother's piano and hopes to take lessons so she can play it again one day.